THE STORY OF
WRITING
AND
PRINTING

by Anita Ganeri

OXFORD UNIVERSITY PRESS

Published in the United States of America by
Oxford University Press, Inc.
198 Madison Avenue
New York, NY 10016

Oxford is a registered trademark of Oxford University Press

Published in the United Kingdom by Evans Brothers Limited
2A Portman Mansions
Chiltern Street
London W1M 1LE

Printed in Hong Kong by Wing King Tong Co. Ltd

Library of Congress Cataloging-in-Publication Data
Ganeri, Anita.
   The story of writing and printing / by Anita Ganeri.
      p. cm. — (Signs of the times)
Includes index
   ISBN 0-19-521256-8
   1. Writing — History — Juvenile literature. 2. Printing — History —
Juvenile literature. I. Title. II. Series: Ganeri, Anita, 1961-
Signs of the times
Z40.G22 1996
652′.09 — dc20   96-14232
                                                  CIP

Acknowledgments

Editor: Karen Ball

Design: Sally Boothroyd

Illustrations: Hardlines and
Ken Brooks

Production: Jenny Mulvanny

With special thanks to Eric Poole, who acted as
consultant on this title.

Acknowledgments

The author and publishers would like to thank the following for permission to reproduce photographs:
Front cover (main picture) Ancient Art and Architecture Collection, (top) Parker Pen UK Ltd., (bottom left) The
Bridgeman Art Library, (bottom right) Ancient Art and Architecture Collection
Back cover Parker Pen UK Ltd.
Title page British Library, The Bridgeman Art Library
page 6 (top) The Bridgeman Art Library, (bottom) Egyptian Museum, Berlin, Werner Forman Archive page 7 (top) The
British Museum, London, Werner Forman Archive, (bottom) Robert Francis, Robert Harding Picture Library page 8
(top) British Museum, London, The Bridgeman Art Library, (bottom left) e.t. archive, (bottom right) Ancient Art and
Architecture Collection page 9 British Museum, London, The Bridgeman Art Library page 10 The Hutchison Library
page 11 Archiv für Kunst und Geschichte, London page 12 (top) Museo Archeologico Nazionale, Werner Forman
Archive, (middle) Ancient Art and Architecture Collection, (bottom) Giraudon, The Bridgeman Art Library page 13 (top
left, top right and bottom) Parker Pen UK Ltd., (middle left) Berol Ltd. page 14 (top) The Bridgeman Art Library,
(bottom) Gerald Cubitt, Bruce Coleman Limited page 15 (top) P. Rauter, Trip, (middle) The Image Bank, (bottom right)
Joseph Devenney, The Image Bank page 16 (top) Mary Evans Picture Library, (bottom) The Louvre Museum, Werner
Forman Archive page 17 (top) e.t. archive, (bottom) Archivo del Stato, Florence, The Bridgeman Art Library page 18
(top) The Bridgeman Art Library, (bottom) Science and Society Picture Library page 19 Archiv für Kunst und Geschichte,
London page 20 (top) The Financial Times, (bottom) Mary Evans Picture Library page 21 (top) International
Newspapers, Robert Harding Picture Library, (bottom) Dr. Charles Henneghien, Bruce Coleman Limited page 22 (top)
Hulton Deutsch Collection, (bottom) Science and Society Picture Library page 23 (top) Helene Rogers, Trip, (bottom)
Olivetti page 24 (top) British Library, The Bridgeman Art Library, (bottom) Mary Evans Picture Library page 25 (top)
Peter Newark's Historical Pictures, (bottom) ZEFA page 26 The British Library page 27 (top) Archiv für Kunst und
Geschichte, London, (bottom) Larry Mulvehill, Science Photo Library page 28 (left) Parker Pen UK Ltd., (top right)
Ancient Art and Architecture Collection, (bottom right) e.t. archive page 29 Mary Evans Picture Library

Contents

READ ALL ABOUT IT

Writing began about 5,500 years ago as a way of keeping accounts and records, and later of passing on news, views, and stories. Before this, people had to rely on what they could remember, and this was not always very accurate. As people began to trade and travel widely, a more practical and reliable system of storing and passing on information was needed.

Sumerian clay tablet

TEMPLE RECORDS

Some of the earliest-known examples of writing are inscriptions found on clay tablets from Sumeria (now in Iraq). The tablets are more than 5,000 years old. They are temple records, listing heads of cattle, sacks of grain, and the numbers of workers (bakers, brewers, blacksmiths, and slaves) employed in various temples.

DIVINE WRITING

In many early civilizations, writing was thought to be a gift from the gods. The ancient Egyptians believed that Thoth, the god of wisdom, created writing and bestowed it on the world. The word *hieroglyphics*, which describes the Egyptian writing system, means "sacred writing."

The Vikings believed that their god Odin invented the runes they wrote with (see page 9).

The Egyptian god Thoth, in baboon form, with a scribe in attendance.

WRITING PRACTICE

As writing developed, its use spread. People wrote down stories, religious and legal texts, historical and scientific works. An ancient Babylonian text tells the story of the hero Gilgamesh and his daring adventures. At first the story was passed on by word of mouth. It was written down about 3,000 years ago on a vast collection of clay tablets.

SIGNPOST

Without writing, we would know very little about the past. Most of our historical evidence comes from ancient writing. From ancient Egyptian records, for example, we know about what people wore, what they ate, what work they did, the battles they fought, whom they married, what their houses looked like (above), and the gods they worshiped. The writing we leave behind today will provide similar information in the distant future.

WRITE NOW

Today, we are surrounded by writing in all shapes, forms, and sizes. Eye-catching advertising billboards and posters (left) try to tempt us to buy things. Millions of newspapers, comic books, magazines, and books are printed and sold every day. Writing plays an essential part in our lives today as a means of information and communication. Can you imagine a world without it?

THE FIRST ALPHABETS

An alphabet is a system of writing, using letters or signs to stand for sounds and parts of words. The first people to write their language down were the Sumerians, who lived in Iraq in about 3500 B.C. They used pictures, then wedge-shaped symbols, to represent words. The first true alphabet, in which individual letters could be joined together to make up words, appeared in Syria in about 1300 B.C. It worked in the same way that our alphabet works today.

WEDGE-SHAPED WORDS

The Sumerians used pictures to stand for words. For example a cow's head meant "cow," a bird meant "bird," and so on. Later, this developed into a system of writing called cuneiform, or "wedge-shaped," because it used symbols made of wedge-shaped strokes to represent words.

HIEROGLYPHIC HANDWRITING

The ancient Egyptians wrote in picture symbols called hieroglyphs. A sign could represent a whole word, a single sound, or part of a longer word. Hieroglyphs

could be written and read from left to right, right to left, or top to bottom. Animal and people signs provided clues about where to start. If they faced left, you read from left to right, and so on. The whole system was so complicated that highly trained scribes were the only ones to understand it. Most Egyptians couldn't read or write!

Egyptian hieroglyphs

Cuneiform was written in wet clay, with a reed cut at an angle at the end. The clay was then baked hard by the sun.

Scribes kept their writing equipment – reed pens and ink – in wooden writing cases.

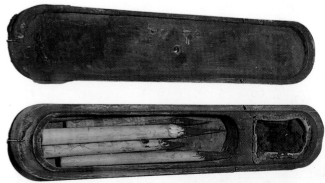

ALL GREEK TO ME

In the 8th century B.C, the ancient Greeks adopted the alphabet of the Phoenicians, a trading people from Lebanon. The Greeks had to add vowels – the Phoenician alphabet only used consonants. At first they wrote from right to left. Then they tried writing "plow-wise," changing direction at the end of each line, like an oxen plowing a field. Eventually, they settled on writing from left to right, which made life a lot easier!

THE ROMANS RULE

A form of the Greek alphabet was adapted for writing Latin, the language of the Romans. During the time of the Roman Empire, the alphabet contained only 22 letters. *J, U, W, Y,* and *Z* were added later. Long after the Romans had come and gone, their alphabet remained. In the Middle Ages, Latin was the language of scholars and the church. The alphabet we use today to write English is based on the Roman alphabet.

Rosetta Stone

BREAKTHROUGH

Hieroglyphs remained a complete mystery until 1822. Then, for the first time, a French linguist, Jean-François Champollion, deciphered the hieroglyphs inscribed on a large stone slab known as the Rosetta Stone. He did this by comparing them to the identical Greek text that also appeared on the stone.

SIGNPOST

The Viking alphabet, or futhark (below), gets its name from its first six letters. It was designed to be carved on wood or stone so the individual letters, or runes, are composed of simple, straight lines. Send your own runic messages, carved on to a slab of clay with a knitting needle. Invent your own runes for letters that did not exist in Viking times.

The 16 letters, or runes, of the Viking alphabet

MODERN ALPHABETS

There are many different writing systems in use today. Some, such as Chinese and Japanese, work in the same way as cuneiform and hieroglyphics. They use symbols, called characters, to represent words or ideas. Most alphabets, however, use individual letters joined into words. Some alphabets, such as Turkish, are phonetic. This means that each letter is pronounced as it is written.

IN FACT...

The longest alphabet is Khmer, from Cambodia, with 74 letters. The shortest is Rotokas, from the Soloman Islands, with just 11 letters. The English alphabet has 26 letters.

ក ខ គ យ
ប ឈ ឬ ច ឍ

Above: some examples of the intricate letters that make up the Khmer alphabet

FULL OF CHARACTER

According to legend, Chinese writing was a gift to an emperor from a magic tortoise he had saved from drowning. Each symbol, or character, stands for a word or idea. Different characters are combined to make different words. To read and write Chinese well, you need to know about 2,000 characters. But there are over 40,000 characters in total. New characters have to be designed for any new ideas or objects that come into the Chinese language.

Chinese calligraphy is a fine art and governed by strict rules.

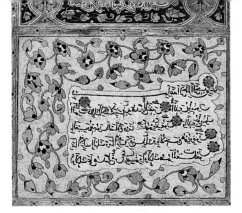

ARABIC ART

Arabic is written from right to left. It has 28 basic letters, with special accents and marks to indicate vowels. Arabic is the language of the Muslim world and of the Koran, the holy book of Islam. No human figures are allowed to be shown in copies of the Koran. The pages are decorated with beautifully drawn letters and words.

BREAKTHROUGH

New alphabets are still being invented for languages that have never been written down before. In the 1840s, a missionary, John Evans, invented a script for the Cree Indians of North America, to make it easier to spread his message. In the 1930s, a script for the Mende language of Sierra Leone was created by a local tailor.

OTHER ALPHABETS

Cyrillic

Cyrillic is the alphabet used to write Russian. It is named after St. Cyril, who preached Christianity to the Russians in the 9th century. It is based on the Greek alphabet.

This line is written in Cyrillic:

Эта строка написана по-русски.

Hebrew

Hebrew is the ancient language of the Bible and the official language of modern Israel. The square script has changed very little over the last 2,000 years. It is written from right to left, and dots and dashes can be used to indicate vowels.

This line is written in Hebrew:

השורה הזאת כתובה בעברית

Devanagari

Devanagari is the alphabet used to write Hindi, the major language of India. It is written from left to right. Each word is made up of letters joined together by a horizontal bar running across the top.

This line is written in Hindi:

यह पंक्ति हिन्दी में लिखी है ।

DOTS AND DASHES

Punctuation marks are symbols that indicate how sentences should be said. In English, for example, a comma (,) means a slight pause. A full stop (.) indicates the end of a sentence. An exclamation mark (!) indicates a tone of surprise or humor. Each language has its own system of punctuation, even if it uses a similar alphabet to another language. English and Spanish use similar alphabets, but the Spanish question mark is written upside down(¿). In Hindi a full stop is written as a vertical bar (I).

PENS AND PENCILS

Early writers did not have the enormous range of pens, pencils, and other writing implements we have at our fingertips today. In the Middle East, where writing began, reeds and rushes grew in many areas. So people cut lengths of reeds, sharpened the ends, dipped them into soot or ink, and used them to write with. Since then, writing has progressed in leaps and bounds. And the need for greater accuracy and speed has led to many improvements in writing instruments. The basic rules behind pens and other tools of the trade, however, have remained much the same.

A Roman girl with her wax writing tablet and stylus

STYLUS STYLE

In Greek and Roman times, metal and bone replaced the reeds of the earliest pens. Writers used styli of bronze, bone, or ivory to scratch letters on to wax panels. The pointed end of the stylus was used for writing with, the blunt end for erasing mistakes!

Roman inkwells. Ink was made from soot and water.

QUILL PENS

The first quill pens were made in about 500 B.C. and were still in use in the 17th and 18th centuries. Quill pens were made from swan or goose feathers, cut into a point at one end to make a nib. This was then dipped in ink. Quill pens were quick and handy to use. The only problem was that they kept going blunt and having to be resharpened.

Quill pens were the most popular writing implements until the 1800s.

BREAKTHROUGH

The inventor of the ballpoint pen (called a biro in England) was, in fact, Ladislao Josef Biro, a Hungarian living in Argentina. He registered his invention in 1938.

NIBS OF STEEL

The first metal nibs were so hard and rigid, they scratched paper to pieces. But, by the mid-1800s, things had improved and steel-nibbed pens became very popular. The first fountain pens used eyedroppers to contain their ink, but the ink kept clotting and clogging up the nib. The first workable fountain pen was produced by an American, Lewis Waterman, in 1884. You can still buy Waterman pens today. One problem remained, however. Every time the pen ran out of ink, it had to be refilled. This could be messy and time-consuming. In the 1950s, an answer was found – the disposable ink cartridge. Once its ink supply was used up, it could be thrown away and a new cartridge inserted.

Lewis Waterman, inventor of the modern fountain pen

PENCIL POWER

Pencils were first made in about 1795. A pencil is a stick of "lead" (it's actually a mixture of clay and graphite), held inside a wooden case. Pencils have different degrees of hardness or softness, indicated by the letters printed on them. Soft pencils (B and 2B) contain more graphite in their lead. Hard pencils (H and 2H) contain more clay.

BALLPOINT PENS

A ballpoint pen has a tiny ball bearing in its writing tip instead of a nib. As you write, the ball bearing gets coated in ink from a tube inside the pen and rolls the ink onto the paper. When the ink runs dry, you can throw away the pen and get a new one. Other cheap, disposable pens include rollerball and fiber-tipped pens.

IN FACT...

Thomas Edison is best known for his invention of the electric light bulb and the phonograph. But another of his more unusual inventions was an electric pen. It was designed to make copies of handwritten documents, but it never really caught on.

Size, shape, nib style, and ink flow are all taken into account when a new pen is designed.

PAPER AND INK

Before paper was invented, people wrote on whatever materials they had at hand. These included wet clay, metal, stone, wood, bark, bamboo, bone, palm leaves, and silk. Greek and Roman schoolchildren practiced their writing on waxed tablets and scraps of pottery. Then it didn't matter if they made mistakes. The first paperlike material was papyrus. It was made from the papyrus reeds that grew in ancient Egypt.

Ancient Chinese writing on bone

PAPYRUS APLENTY

Papyrus was made from reeds that grew along the Nile River. Thin strips were cut from the plant stems and overlapped to form layers. These were beaten together into sheets and dried in the sun. Then the sheets were pasted together to make a long roll for writing on. The Egyptian government controlled the papyrus trade and made a lot of money from papyrus exports.

PAGES OF PARCHMENT

So much papyrus was produced that supplies began to run low. A new writing material was needed. This was parchment, made from the skins of goats, sheep, or calves. The skins were washed, soaked in lime, and scraped clean. Then they were stretched and scraped again to give a really smooth surface for writing on.

Papyrus plants grew on plantations along the Nile River. They were used to make writing sheets, sails, and mats.

Handmade paper drying in the sun

PAPER-MAKING PROGRESS

Paper has been the most important writing material for hundreds of years and remains so today. It has made writing and printing quicker, easier, and cheaper. Until the 19th century, most paper was made by hand, from linen rags. Today, it is made in special paper mills, mainly from coniferous trees such as spruce and pine.

Paper as we know it today was invented in China in 105 A.D. But the Chinese kept their discovery secret until the 7th century, when it spread to Japan, Arabia, and Europe. The Arabs learned to make paper from Chinese prisoners of war. This first paper was made from bamboo, bark, or rags that were mixed into a pulp and spread out to dry in sheets.

WHAT'S IN INK?

The Egyptians and Chinese made thick, black ink from soot, water, and gum. The gum helped the ink to stick to the page. The Egyptians also used red ink, made of crushed minerals and water, for titles, headings, and the names of gods. In the Middle Ages, many ingredients went into ink, including iron ore and oak apples. Most modern inks are produced synthetically. Many of them contain acrylic, a synthetic, glasslike material. Today, there is a huge variety of inks available in many different colors. You can even buy fluorescent inks for when you want to read in the dark!

A modern paper mill

IN FACT...

A paper clip is made of a piece of wire bent into two loops. It looks incredibly simple but is an ingenious way of pinning loose sheets of paper together without damaging them. The inventor of the paper clip was a Norwegian, Johann Vaaler. He patented his design in 1900.

BOOKS BY HAND

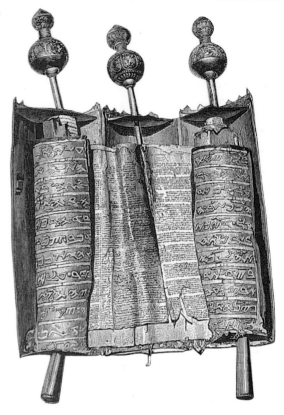

An ancient Hebrew scroll

Until the invention of printing, every book had to be copied out and illustrated by hand. Because books took months or even years to complete, very few were produced and these were very expensive. University students in the Middle Ages had to copy out the textbooks they needed. The originals were kept firmly chained to the library shelves to prevent theft!

BOOK IN A SCROLL

The earliest books were written on clay tablets, then on rolls of papyrus or parchment, called scrolls. Scrolls were used by the Egyptians, Greeks, and Romans and remained the usual form of book until the 4th century A.D. Egyptian scrolls were up to 131 feet (40 meters) long. The text was written in columns so you could unroll and read the scroll column by column. Scrolls are still used today in synagogues, where special scribes are employed to write the Hebrew scriptures out by hand.

SCRIBES AT WORK

In the past, many people did not learn to read or write. It was not only the working classes who were unable to understand the written word – many rulers and people of high birth had to employ scribes. Scribes were professional writers who spent years at special writing schools, practicing their trade. In ancient Egypt, these schools were very strict. Trainee scribes were beaten or even sent to prison if they made mistakes! If they did well, however, they were guaranteed a good job.

In Egypt, scribes were well respected and well paid.

16

BREAKTHROUGH

In the 4th century A.D., books changed shape. The scroll was replaced by the codex, which is similar to the type of book we have today, where the pages are between two covers. It was much more convenient to read and write in. Try making your own scroll and codex to compare which is easiest to use.

ILLUMINATED MANUSCRIPTS

In the Middle Ages, each monastery had its own scriptorium, a room where the monks produced copies of the Bible, prayer books, and other religious works. These manuscripts were works of art, beautifully designed and decorated. The monks specialized in exquisite "illuminated" letters, colored with bright reds, greens, blues, and even gold leaf.

An illuminated page from an early Bible

A medieval codex

WRITING GUILDS

From the Middle Ages onward, the demand for books grew and grew. Some professional scribes formed groups, or guilds, that worked separately from the monasteries. They copied out official documents and books on subjects such as cooking, medicine, astronomy, and love poetry for wealthy clients.

IN FACT...

The word *manuscript* comes from two Latin words, *manus* and *scriptum*, meaning "hand" and "writing." This is because all early manuscripts were written by hand.

THE FIRST PRINTERS

Handwritten books looked very beautiful but they were expensive and time-consuming to produce. As the demand for books grew, a new, more efficient way of producing cheaper books in greater numbers was called for. In the 15th century, the first printed books were made in Europe. Things would never be the same again.

ON YOUR BLOCKS

The Chinese were using carved seals to stamp official documents long before printing reached Europe. Later, they invented block printing, using wooden blocks to print whole pages of text. Characters were cut into the wood so they stood out in relief and in reverse. Then the block was inked and a sheet of paper pressed down on it so the text was printed the right way around.

An early Chinese block-printed bank note

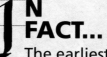

IN FACT...

The earliest-known printed book is a block-printed Chinese scroll, called the *Diamond Sutra*. Printed in the late 9th century, it is a Buddhist prayer scroll, illustrated with scenes from the Buddha's life.

MOVABLE TYPE

The next major printing breakthrough was the invention of movable type. Individual letters were carved onto separate blocks that could be grouped into words, lines, and pages. The letters could be used again and again, unlike the earlier woodblocks. Movable type was invented in China in the 1040s but took another 400 years to reach Europe.

Early bronze printing blocks from Korea. The first Chinese printing blocks were made from clay.

JOHANNES GUTENBERG

Johannes Gutenberg, a German goldsmith, was the first European to use movable type. In about 1438, he invented a mold for making large amounts of type, quickly and cheaply, from molten metal. Gutenberg also devised the first printing press by adapting a hand-operated wooden wine press. This pressed a sheet of paper on to a tray of inked type to print a page.

GUTENBERG'S BIBLE

In 1455, after two years' hard work, Gutenberg produced the world's first ever printed Bible. The Bible is in two volumes, of 600 pages each. About 160 copies were printed. The colors and illustrations were added later by hand.

A page from the Gutenberg Bible

SIGNPOST

The first printers faced tough competition from the writers' guilds. To get their printed books accepted, they tried to make them as much like handwritten copies as possible. Many used typefaces based on the style of writing in handwritten manuscripts. Gutenberg, for example, printed his Bible in Gothic script, similar to the script on the right, a handwriting style that was popular in Germany at that time.

Schreiben *means "to write" in German.*

MODERN METHODS

Gutenberg's ideas spread quickly and print shops grew up all over Europe. Incredibly, the printing press he devised was used, almost unchanged, right up to the beginning of the 19th century. Then the new machinery of the time helped to improve and speed up the printing process still further. The 20th century has seen another leap forward, with computer technology revolutionizing printing and publishing.

A modern printing press

STEAM PRESSES

In 1810 a German named Frederick König improved on Gutenberg's hand-operated printing press by adding steam power. This doubled the speed at which pages of print could be produced, from 200 to 400 an hour. Rollers automatically inked the tray of type.

A steam-powered printing press, 1877

ROTARY PRESSES

In 1845 the printing process was made even quicker with the development of the first successful rotary press, invented by an American, Richard Hoe. This first rotary press had two cylinders. The paper was rolled around one cylinder and the type around the other. Huge rotary presses are still used today to print newspapers and books. The text and pictures that make up the pages are photographed onto special metal printing plates. These are wound around the rollers. Paper and ink are fed into the press to produce the printed pages.

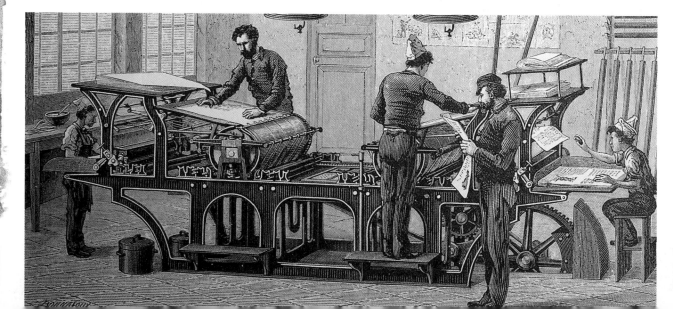

IN FACT...

The first newspaper appeared in Roman times. It was a handwritten news sheet called the *Acta Diurna* or "Daily News." It was hung up around the city and contained battle reports; the results of gladiator contests; and a register of births, deaths, and marriages. The most widely read modern newspaper is the Japanese *Yomiuri Shimbun*. Over 14 million people read it every day.

PRINTING COLORS

Until 1457 color was added to books by hand after they had been printed. Then two German printers invented a way of inking some parts of the type in a second, different color. In 1719 another German printer realized that any color could be made by mixing three basic colors – red, yellow, and blue. In modern four-color printing, each color is separated into magenta (red), yellow, cyan (blue), and black. An image is scanned and photographed by a machine that separates the colors. Then a printing plate is made of each color. These are printed on top of one another to reproduce the colors of the original.

BREAKTHROUGH

In the 1880s two machines, the Linotype and the Monotype, were invented. Both could set (arrange) type automatically. Before this, type was set by hand, a very slow, very tedious job. In 1939 the photocomposing machine was invented. It set type photographically on paper. This was followed in 1965 by Digiset, a computer-controlled typesetting system. Most typesetting today, including this book, is done by computer.

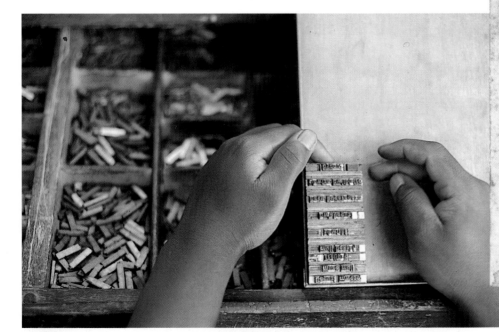

Setting lines of type by hand

WRITING MACHINES

From reed pens, styli, and quills to typewriters and word processors, writing equipment has come a long way since the Sumerians inscribed their clay tablets. The 19th century saw the invention of writing machines, including typewriters. They were slow to catch on, as office clerks could often produce documents more quickly and neatly by hand than on early typewriters. Today, however, typewriters and word processors are an everyday part of office life.

An office typing pool in the 1930s

THE FIRST TYPISTS

The first typewriter was invented in 1808 by an Italian, Pellegrino Turri. He devised it to enable a blind friend to write her own letters. The first modern manual typewriter was produced in 1874 for the Remington Company in the United States. It was very large, very heavy, and very hard to use.

TOUCH TYPING

The first electric typewriters appeared in 1902, making typing much quicker and easier. Modern electronic typewriters are even more convenient. They contain silicon chips that allow them to correct words, underline, set margins, and so on automatically. They can store large chunks of text in their memory and type them out at the touch of a key.

An early electric typewriter

SIGNPOST

There are practical problems to overcome when designing keyboards for different languages. An English-language typewriter needs only 50 keys, for example, but some of the first Japanese typewriters needed space for at least 2,000 symbols. Fortunately, modern word processors can now store all these Japanese symbols in their memories.

BREAKTHROUGH

In 1964 the first word processor was produced by IBM, and it revolutionized typing. A word processor is a cross between a typewriter and a computer. You can check and correct text and spelling on-screen before printing it out. This is much easier than correcting a typewritten page or having to start all over again.

A modern newsroom

A modern fax machine

DESKTOP PUBLISHING

Desktop publishing (DTP) is the latest innovation in writing machine technology. It allows you to write, design, and typeset a whole book or newspaper on-screen, at one time and without leaving your desk! All this information can then be stored on disk and sent straight to the printer.

FAX FANTASTIC

Fax machines send pictures and text over a telephone line. They are used by journalists, weather forecasters, and anyone who needs instant information. A page takes less than a minute to transmit. Faxes were first used in the 1900s, but it is in the last 10 years that they have made a real impact on office life.

BOOKS FOR ALL

The first libraries were established in Babylonia and Egypt more than 4,000 years ago, to store great collections of clay tablets and papyrus scrolls. There were many libraries in ancient Greece and Rome, too. These ancient libraries were usually set up by the king or emperor. In the Middle Ages, libraries were privately owned, by churches, monasteries, universities, and wealthy individuals. The first free public libraries were not opened until the early 1900s.

A personal, portable library from the 17th century

LIBRARY OF CLAY

One of the earliest libraries was set up by King Ashurbanipal of Assyria in the 7th century B.C. The library contained about 22,000 clay tablets, including histories of people and events dating back to the 23rd century B.C., grammar books and dictionaries, and a huge number of stories and poems.

SHELVES OF SCROLLS

The library in Alexandria, Egypt, (left) was the most famous of its time. Built in 305 B.C., it contained half a million papyrus scrolls, neatly labeled and stacked on shelves. There were copies of every important work in Greek and translations of many foreign books. Scholars came from all over the world to study in the library.

The Alexandria library in Egypt

BREAKTHROUGH

In the 18th and 19th centuries, some private libraries were opened to the public. But people had to pay to borrow the books. The first free public libraries were opened at the start of this century.

A 19th-century lending library

LARGEST LIBRARY

The world's largest library is the Library of Congress in Washington, D.C. Founded in 1800, it now contains 28 million books and pamphlets, arranged on 583 miles (940 kilometers) of shelves. The British Library in London is the biggest library in Britain, with more than 18 million books.

The huge main reading room in the Library of Congress, Washington, D.C.

BOOK BUYING

Today, you can buy books everywhere, in bookstores, at train stations, in supermarkets. They are produced by publishers and sold to bookstores to sell to you. In the early days of printing, printers sold their books themselves, often through street vendors. Some of today's publishers started out as book printers. The world's best-selling book is the Bible. Millions of copies have been printed, in more than 300 languages.

IN FACT...

Perhaps the most overdue library book was borrowed from the Sidney Sussex College library in Cambridge, England, in 1667. It was found and returned to the library some 288 years later. Fortunately, the fine was dropped!

Using Lettering

There are many different styles of writing and lettering. Depending on their use, they may be plain, decorative, dramatic, or delicate. The different designs of type (the letters used in printing) are called typefaces. Early typefaces were based on handwriting styles. Since then, thousands of typefaces have been designed and are still being designed.

A NAME TO THE FACE

Each typeface has a name and particular features. This book is set in Garamond which is clear and easy to read. Titles and headings are set in a heavier "weight" of type, called **bold**, to make them stand out. The normal weight of type is called roman. *Italics* are also used for emphasis. Different sizes of type are used for the main headings, introductory text, and paragraph text. All these things have to be worked out when the book is designed.

Here are examples of the alphabet in capital letters using four different typefaces:

A B C D E F G H I
J K L M N O P Q
R S T U V W X Y Z
(Helvetica)

A B C D E F G H I
J K L M N O P Q
R S T U V W X Y Z
(Flora medium)

A B C D E F G H I
J K L M N O P Q
R S T U V W X Y Z
(Benguiat)

*A B C D E F G H I
J K L M N O P Q
R S T U V W X Y Z*
(Zapf Chancery)

TORY'S TYPEFACE

In the early 16th century, Geoffroy Tory, a French designer, devised an extraordinary typeface (below). He used the proportions of the human body to shape each letter.

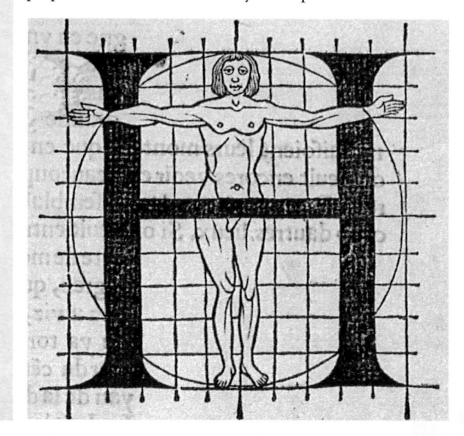

Modern graffiti

ROMAN GRAFFITI

Graffiti means the words and drawings scribbled, scrawled, or sprayed on to walls, often in anger or protest. But graffiti is nothing new. The walls of the Roman town of Pompeii were covered in graffiti, including offers of rewards for the return of stolen goods.

THE ART OF WRITING

The art of beautiful handwriting is called calligraphy. Calligraphers use special pens, brushes, and inks to produce highly decorative lettering for invitations, labels, greeting cards, and so on. Arabic calligraphy is used to decorate copies of the Koran (see page 11). In China and Southeast Asia, master calligraphers are highly respected. You can buy books on calligraphy or calligraphy kits from a bookstore or art supply store, if you want to give it a try yourself.

BREAKTHROUGH

In 1824 a new form of lettering was devised by a Frenchman, Louis Braille. It was designed for blind people to read and is still used today. Each letter of the Braille alphabet is a pattern of raised dots that can be felt with the fingers. It is typed on a special Braille typewriter.

SIGNPOST

Shorthand is a way of writing quickly using symbols to stand for letters. The Romans invented a form of shorthand to record political speeches. Shorthand systems today use dots, dashes, curves, and straight lines to represent sounds, rather than letters. Try devising your own shorthand system. How many words can you write in a minute? The line below is British shorthand. It says "This line is written in shorthand."

TIMELINE

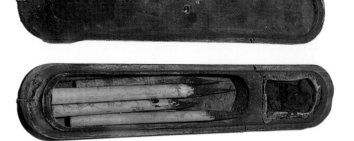

B.C.
- **3500** Writing begins in Sumeria
- **3000** Hieroglyphs are used in Egypt
- **2100** Oldest medical text, Sumeria
- **2000** First libraries, Babylonia
- **1300** First true alphabet, Syria
- **1200** Chinese writing develops
- **800** The Greeks adopt and adapt the Phoenician alphabet
- **500** First quill pens used in Europe
- **400** The Etruscans adopt a form of the Greek alphabet that becomes the basis for the Roman alphabet
- **305** Library built at Alexandria

A.D.
- **105** First true paper made in China
- **200** Viking runes develop
- **400** Codex book form introduced
- **868** First printed book, the *Diamond Sutra*, produced in China
- **900s** Illuminated manuscripts begin to be produced in monasteries
- **1040s** Movable type invented in China
- **1438** Gutenberg invents movable type and the printing press in Europe
- **1455** Gutenberg's Bible appears
- **1719** Full-color printing invented
- **1795** First pencils made
- **1810** First steam-powered printing press
- **1822** Rosetta Stone deciphered
- **1845** First rotary printing press
- **1874** First modern manual typewriter
- **1884** First working fountain pen
- **1886** Linotype machine invented
- **1887** Monotype machine invented
- **1900** Paper clip invented
- **1938** First ballpoint pens
- **1939** Photocomposing machine invented
- **1964** First word processor
- **1965** Digiset invented
- **1980s** Desktop publishing widely used

GLOSSARY

Alphabet A writing system that uses letters to stand for sounds and for parts of words.

Characters Symbols that represent ideas or words in a language such as Chinese or Japanese.

Codex A book made of sheets of parchment or paper bound together between two covers.

Cuneiform The wedge-shaped writing devised by the ancient Sumerians.

Futhark The Viking alphabet.

Hieroglyphs The picture symbols used in the ancient Egyptian writing system.

Illuminated Illustrated or decorated.

Lead The stick of clay and graphite inside a pencil.

Papyrus A paperlike material made of reeds in ancient Egypt.

Parchment A material for writing on made of animal skin.

Phonetic Describes letters that are pronounced as they are written.

Punctuation Marks or accents that show you how to say a sentence — for example, where to pause, when to stop, and so on.

Quill pens Ink pens made of large feathers.

Runes The sharp, angular symbols forming the letters of the futhark, or Viking alphabet.

Scribes Highly trained professional writers.

Scriptorium A room in a monastery where monks worked on illuminated manuscripts in the Middle Ages.

Scrolls Long rolls of papyrus, parchment, or paper used in the past as books.

Stylus Early writing instrument, made of rods of bone, wood, or metal. Used for writing on wax tablets.

Type The sets of letters that are used in printing.

Typefaces The different styles or designs of type.

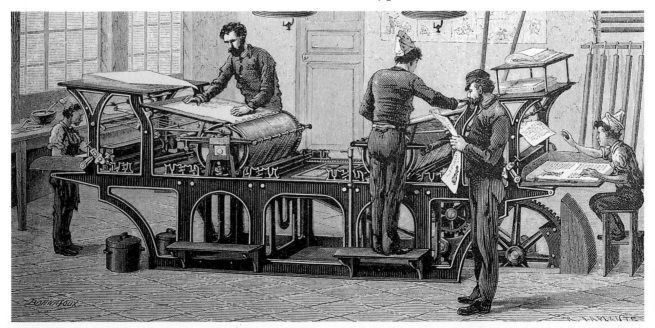

INDEX